Atelier 13
Research and Coherence

Preface by
Nicole Roux Loupiac
Jean Philippe Loupiac
Introduction by
Paolo Righetti

l'ARCAEDIZIONI

Photographic Credits

Abbadie, 24 (photo 1), 25 (photo 2), 34, 37, 38, 39, 42

Berthelemy, 74

Cesar, 14, 16, 17, 44, 45, 46, 47, 54, 55, 56, 57, 58, 59, 63, 64, 65, 66, 67, 75, 82, 83, 95 (photos 1,3)

J. Ph. Loupiac - Fabre, 15, 20, 21, 24 (photo 2), 25 (photo 1), 26, 27, 30, 31, 35, 36, 43, 50, 51, 62, 70, 71, 78, 79, 86, 87, 94, 95 (photo 2)

Perspective
A. Buenomo, 91

Chief Editor of Collection
Maurizio Vitta

Publishing Coordinator
Franca Rottola

Editorial Staff
Cristina Rota

Graphic Design
Paola Polastri

Editing
Martyn J. Anderson

Colour-separation
LitofilmsItalia, Bergamo

Printing
Bolis Poligrafiche SpA, Azzano San Paolo (BG)

First published November 2002

Copyright 2002
by l'Arca Edizioni

ISBN 88-7838-118-7

Contents

Research and Coherence
by Nicole Roux Loupiac and Jean Philippe Loupiac

Doing architecture and town-planning means creating a vision of the world in which we live and providing your own contribution to it; or in other words, it is like injecting a healthy dose of coherence.

The problem lies in the pluralism of architecture, and the complexity and diversity of the parameters whose synthesis it must ensure: meeting programme needs, fulfilling cultural, symbolic and social expectations, as well as unexpressed aspirations, and catering for site location, technical and economic restrictions and normative/building constraints.

This involves more than just applying each of these parameters: success is more than just the sum of these elements.

Creating coherence means creating bonds between separate elements to produce meaning; this entails a constant battle against one-track thought, the pigeonholing of knowledge into individual categories; this calls for transversal cross-the-board thoughts and an awareness that space may be captured on various scales.

Architecture belongs to the urban, rural or natural landscape, but what is more important is the use made of it. It is made for people.

Its socio-political vocation connects it to users and inhabitants, which means it must be more than just useful; spaces must convey feelings; "man lives poetically" so Holderlïn said. Structures, materials, colours and light all participate in the poetics of space.

Finally, architecture is both an intellectual act deriving from thought – architecture and experimentation cannot be separated, they are so closely related – and a physical act imposed by matter. The building site and meticulous construction of details are part of architecture. Coherence derives from control over design and its implementation. As an ethical calling, making architecture means seeking truth or, in other words, searching for our very self.

A Stylistic Verve

by Paolo Righetti

The best way to analyse the elaborate, wide-ranging work of Atelier 13, the Toulouse-based firm founded and run by Jean Philippe Loupiac and Nicole Roux Loupiac, and bring it into relation with both local and international architecture is to compare it to how French architecture has developed over recent decades. French architecture draws heavily on differences and distinctive features to lay the foundations for the kind of authoritative autonomy dominating the international scene, not only as regards its architectural experimentation but also its widespread popularity (the land has almost been "pulverised") and the system of managing resources and hence interacting with the clientele.

We must inevitably take a quick glance back over those key moments in architectural debate in the 1960s-70s, the experimentation carried out by the *avant-gardes*, and the constant shift in balance from architecture to the landscape, from buildings to the city and vice-versa, if we are to grasp their repercussions on modern-day culture. These are the realms in which the leading exponents of architecture in both the present day and recent past in France began their explorations, from Nouvel to Portzamparc, from Ciriani to Sarfati, and from Tschumi to Chemetov.

The death of the great master Le Corbusier may be taken as the waterline marking the transition to a long period of debate, whose first consequence was the reaction against the Modern and the Academy, the first victims of this period of re-thinking and experimentation. The roots of the most concrete experimentation on a truly practical level, such as the Grands Ensembles, ZUPs, Villes Nouvelles, and certain more theoretical experiments, are all deeply entrenched in a critique of the Charter of Athens and the crisis in the Ecole des Beaux-Arts.

This includes the so-called visionary and futuristic cities (bridge-city, floating city, flower city, and subterranean town-planning) that came into being at the same time as Archigram's work in England and the Metabolists in Japan, or sculptural architecture that took its inspiration from Niemeyer, Saarinen and even Le Corbusier's own later works.

This same vein of experimentation also encompasses the proliferating architecture of the late-1960s by Candilis and the young Bernard Tschumi or the neo-monumental architecture of megastructures, in which house and road merge together according to the Town Design theories laid down by Kevin Lynch, notably in the work of Henri E. Ciriani or Jean Bossu.

This period of experimentation, that often never got beyond the drawing board but in some cases was indeed transformed into actual constructions, also saw the emergence of an approach to design and culture in general in which, unlike in other countries, set no clear boundary between architecture, the land, town-planning and infrastructures, and hence between the various categories of people responsible for them, splitting the profession into lots of different sections working in parallel.

Architects, engineers and town-planners worked in unison without almost ever overlapping, interacting or exchanging roles.

In France, on the contrary, architectural tension and attention was being increasingly focused on issues and works which in other contexts might be seen as verging on industrial production. Architects ended up handling absolutely anything altering the territory in the widest possible sense, including architecture, infrastructures, technical constructs, town-planning, roads, bridges plants. It was realised that the way the territory is perceived is very often influenced by works which would not usually fall under the immediate jurisdiction of architecture and, therefore, were exempt from any control over the way they knit stylistically and aesthetically into the anthropised landscape.

In a state of affairs like this, there is a first important premise in analysing Atelier 13's work, to which a second may be added based again on the remarks just made about the experiments of the *avant-gardes*.

The premise in question does not so much refer to architectural objects as the scale and scope of architecture itself. The analysing and experimenting with the urban scale of architecture undertaken by the architectural *avant-gardes* and continued right down to the present day, and the reiterated leap in scale between architecture and the city, resulted in a definite type of practice, a way of reading the city's close relations with architecture, that never fails to take location into account.

Not as a forced academic reading of context but as an intimate way of relating architecture to its territories.

A distinctive feature of Atelier 13's work is the firm's architectural bonds with a region or well-defined territory. Such in-depth knowledge of these contexts guarantees certain shared principles of conformance to an urban/territorial system are carefully abided by. The geographical bounds in which Atelier 13 operates are certainly highly distinctive in a number of ways. Most importantly, certain relations to Toulouse's important industrial heritage, notably the aerospace industry. A socio-economic system that at least superficially evokes a sense of technological efficiency and wealth, scientific research and experimentation. This has resulted in a number of high-profile clients interested in every aspect of the built environment in harmony with the premises already stated.

A territory that also has the important characteristic of being a sort of in-between land relating administratively, culturally and geographically with the architectural world of the "north" and with Mediterranean tradition (variegated but distinctive and interrelated).

A distinctive feature that the region holds dear and that down the ages has developed into something clearly identifiable and detectable as you move across the territory.

Working on these important assumptions, let's try and take a closer look at Atelier 13's own work.

Their approach to design can only really be properly understood if we acknowledge three recurring design situations resulting in an interweaving of common practices and specific approaches.

The first concerns territorial or urban scale works, whose projects are designed to fit into smoothly-knit areas linked, for instance, to existing or expanding settlements or to the construction of infrastructural works.

The second, on the other hand, refers to architectural works scaled to what already exists, usually involving the redevelopment of old buildings and, at times, the addition of new constructions. Finally, the third deals with works scaled to new architecture, working on areas entirely free to be built on or replacements of existing buildings.

It is useful to note these three macro-categories of works because Atelier 13 draws on common approaches and tailor-made strategies for them all, which are most interesting to analyse and underline.

Atelier 13's approach to design begins with contextual planning, an urban or micro-urban framing in place that expresses the kind of analysis of setting bringing a design in line with the complexities, vocations, specific features and evolutionary history of the land in which it is located. Powerful relations to the geographical area of Toulouse play an important role, allowing the firm to be extremely clear sighted in its analysis, thanks to this in-depth knowledge of the local town-planning and environmental structures. In some case the contextual planning work is followed by direct architectural action carried out by Atelier 13 itself, but in others it just paves the way for design work by other firms that then construct their own individual works of architecture. In such cases the work is designed like a project for projects involving micro town-planning accompanied by a grid of structural and morphological constraints for subsequent projects to conform to.

There is also involvement in actually implementing the decisions made and solutions provided by other experts, so as to ensure the entire operation is carefully controlled according to plan.

On the same scale we also have infrastructural design projects for which the same remarks apply in relation to powerful bonds with the territory, and it is worth underlining the attention both architects and their clients pay to operations like this in France. Once again it is important to re-emphasise the premises made at the beginning of our analysis as a useful way of understanding this distinctly French approach to buildings and constructions like this.

Firstly, placing infrastructural work in the hands of architects shows just what an important role architects and architecture have gained in France down the years. There is perhaps no need to mention the law passed on 3rd January 1977 stipulating that architects must be used for all major design work, truly making architecture part of the nation's heritage.

Secondly, constant interaction between architectural and urban design (the heart of plenty of the *avant-garde* experiments we have referred to) now means that the ability to work with different ways of thinking as if they belonged to the same realms and were governed by the same rules seems to be in French architects' DNA. From Le Corbusier's *rue corridor* to Jean Bossu's residential street, roads, paths and ways have always been analysed in great depth and linked to architectural discourse. This means that Atelier 13 treats road infrastructures, viaducts, and outside landscaping designs as genuine works of architecture, paying careful attention to spaces, signs and other emerging features representing elements of carefully gauged continuity and discontinuity in the dynamic perception of these works designed in close harmony with their surroundings, even though they may often only be glimpsed while speeding by in a car.

The action Atelier 13 takes on the existing builtscape once again rests heavily on a careful reading and analysis of the architecture under consideration.

Deep knowledge of the buildings they will eventually be working on allows the architects to pinpoint the functional/morphological features that must be placed at the very focus of their design work, as well as other elements of less obvious importance or which might even conflict with a functional/technological salvaging of the buildings. The purpose of this type of work is almost to blend the new into the old, stitching the evolutionary history of the works of architecture involved neatly back together, without however neglecting to give a clear and clean identity to the fresh design input.

This explains why such careful attention is focused on the design of solutions, right down to their detailed components, where the sense of continuity is expressed by using the original materials (iron rather than metal fixtures, even though the latter are now more widely used) salvaged as part of a more up-to-date building approach. The functionality of the stylistic/distributional features and the preference for absolutely cutting-edge technological and plant-engineering solutions represent, in these cases, the absolute minimum requirements for the buildings they work on. This is part of a clear awareness that a revamped building brought back to life must be as functional and comfortable any new work of architecture.

Atelier 13's new designs move beyond mere contextual interpretation, which nonetheless is still a crucial aspect of their work, to introduce greater freedom to experiment and carry out research. This greater freedom associated with the construction of new works of architecture, that do not bring with them the legacy of powerful morphological/functional bonds associated with the other categories previously examined, allows the team to tackle issues that actually take the form of statements about both contemporary architecture in general and specifically local conditions in particular.

Contrast and counterbalance provide, for instance, a means of bringing lightness and material substance into dialectical relation, expressed by allowing some of the most transparent and light glass structures available to interact with sizeable blank masses, perhaps even clad with copper.

Complexity is sometimes also introduced evoking that sort of intermediate ground in French architecture we mentioned earlier. A sort of complexity that inhabits a land somewhere between the Mediterranean and northern Europe, an interesting matter of contrasts, a form of cross-eyed culture focusing on these two different historical realities. Complexity expressed, for instance, by dipping into a much larger pot of materials than those available to architects working in the capital.

Or perhaps this is just a way of escaping the usual bracketing into pre-defined, trendy architectural categories, so as to be free to opt for solutions deriving directly from

the design, without being forced into a cultural corner. Options freely chosen from aesthetic/morphological solutions that can be traced back to minimalism rather than deconstructivism or high tech, but which actually manage to cross the very concept of classification to be just what a certain work of architecture is really looking for.

Atelier 13 has chosen a heavy approach to its work and labours.

An approach reconciling philosophical respect for historical, geographical and cultural context with a stylistic verve that is neither mimetic or yielding, but on the contrary full of character and independence. This is certainly a difficult approach in which it is most important to control this balance through close coherence to principles, practices and individual actions emerging from carefully layered work. An approach that keeps its options open, crossing over constantly with research rather than fossilising into a system.

Finally, it is a method that controls all these characteristics by working on a transversal professional basis. Architecture is always treated as a service in which all these forms of complexity never lose sight of the user or recipient of these works, the person using them, living in them and bringing them to life, who is actually the real focus of attention.

Works

Motorway
Maintenance
Centre

This building is functionally linked to the infrastructural context, and notably to the A64 motorway. This is the focus of the maintenance and material storage facilities serving the motorway. The complex covers over two thousand square metres, most of which are taken up by workshops and laboratories, while about a tenth of the space serves office purposes. The building also holds a small police station covering about sixty square metres. Halfway between the motorway exits at Muret and Martres Tolosane, the project area is situated on the ring road of the Carbonne motorway junction. The complex encompasses an old industrial building which has been converted and knit into the new architecture. This factory building is composed of two blocks hinged together by a cylindrical structure. The old reconverted building houses the laboratories and workshops, while the cylindrical building holds the public safety unit and the office meeting rooms, also found in the adjacent block but running in the opposite direction. The linear buildings have facades clad with pressed steel panels, while the cylindrical hinging structure is made of precast concrete.

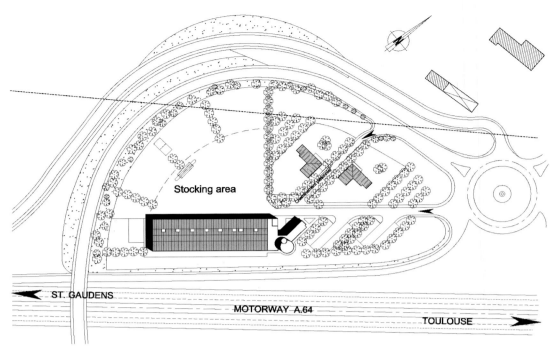

Stocking area

MOTORWAY A.64

TOULOUSE

Site plan.

Below, the police station
control tower
is a symbolic gesture.
Opposite page,
the building stands
alongside the motorway,
with the servicing and
storage areas of
motorway maintenance
products at its rear.
In addition, the unit
is completed
by landscaping
improvements.

Views of the rear facade
of linear building,
clad with pressed steel
panels.

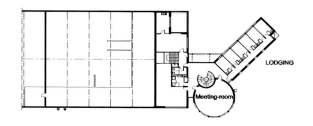

Main floor plan.

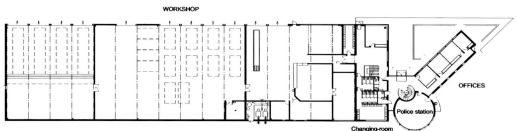

Ground floor plan.

Below, the north
entrance giving access
to the cylinder hosting
the Police Station
and the meeting room.

CNES
Space Centre

In 1962, France affirms her ambition in the space domain, and creates the CNES: the National Space Study Centre. In 1968, the CNES settles in Toulouse in the Rangueil Scientific Complex where it covers an area of 56 hectares at the south-east entrance of the city. Twenty years later, it faced needs of growth, and traffic, parking and architectural image problems. A general rethinking was required to manage the development and to create a fresh architectural identity and awareness of environmental issues. A competition between concept teams was then organised by the establishment. Atelier 13 - prize winner - proposed a directing plan with urban planning rules and an architectural charter, applying for new constructions or existing buildings.

In the directing plan, the roads follow a square grid which define plots 120 to 150 metres long.

Moreover the directing plan treats open spaces which contains separete plans for: landscape, planting and technologic garden; traffic and parking; walkways and lighting with a particular design for the Main Axis.

The architectural charter defines an architectural vocabulary, a building typology with volume envelopes capable of absorbing different programs: offices, laboratories, experiment halls, workshops, etc. These volumes have square plans 30,60 metres long, structured into sub-units of 3,60 or 7,20 on plans, volumes and facades.

For the facades, a range of possible materials has been chosen: prefab concrete panels for technical buildings; grey or white aluminium panels for the other buildings.

Only blue – the official colour of the CNES – can be very sparingly used. The global scheme is put in practice by different architects, but Atelier 13 supervises projects to be sure the documents are respected and exerces control by taking part in the juries for the different competitions.

A tough task that eventually developed into a sort of project for other projects, sensing what repercussions the different approaches would have and immediatly correcting possible distorsions to the overall plan.

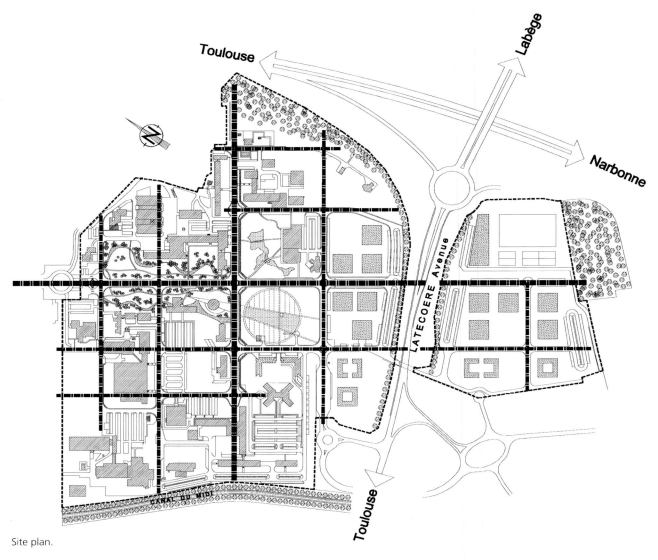

Site plan.

Stainless steel lighting masts stake the site main axis pavements having been removed, walkways now pass through planted areas. They are made of deactivated concrete and you can find old antennas or exposed radars.

Bottom, parking areas, which are separated from the pathways by a planted hedge, have been created along the secondary axes.

South Entrance

ASF – Ministry of Public Works,
Transport and Housing

T his is a 14-metre-high monumental complex that crosses the highway and SNCF line, 6,5 metres above the road level. The main plan provides for a large central pool of water and two roundabouts, perceptually connected by the use of cypress-tree landscaping. Amongst other things, the clients and architects set themselves the task of trying to humanise this setting which, like in many other places like this, is rather hostile, instilling it with a more familiar and urban nature. The reinforced concrete work is a bridge 35 m long, divided into two spans of 18,5 m and 16,5 m, at 14 m high.

Large embankments and reinforced infills form the link with existing paths. The cladding is also made of prefabricated reinforced concrete enriched with different coloured marble grey, designed in the form of coloured strips in order to play down its height. The construction is framed in a sort of hollow egg-shaped cornice combined with a reflective blue band.

The landscape features a spiral design that gives the place a definite geometric form and follows the motorist's movement.

A monument to the French Resistance stands in the middle of the design as a sort of reference point. Twelve "rays" of cypress-trees project out from the monument interacting with the curved road. Stumps shaped like truncated pyramids hold the end cypress in each row.

The project results in a system whose independence as a new and comprehensible structure carefully fits in perceptually with other features along the road from Toulouse to Muret.

Above, Langlade work.
Left, Bordelongue
exchanger punctuated
with pyramid trunks.
Cypresses geometrize
the space. In the
center, the Resistance
Monument.

Langlade bridge piers
are reflected in the water.
Below, the SNCF railway
line goes diagonally
across the Langlade work.

Below, the pyramid
trunks follow the
exchanger movement,
thereby giving it a
strong image.

A curved concrete work is located on the exchanger. Note the concrete and granulate marble piers.

Bridge upon the Dordogne River

Dordogne County Council

This project is the result of a competition. The existing work - an overhanging bridge – connects two municipalities: Port Sainte Foy in Dordogne and Sainte Foy la Grande in Gironde. Due to the high traffic, this work had become unusable and its demolition was foreseen. In order to give the work an urban character and make pedestrian crossing possible, a new construction integrating the historic dimension of the area was necessary. As a consequence, it has been decided to maintain both the existing stone sides of the river and to create the thinnest possible line between the two banks. The pedestrian pathway overhangs the river, thereby providing the necessary thinness of the slab.

Left, without mimicry,
the concrete piers
and their marked joints
harmonize with the
stone sides and likewise
the bridge lighting
maintains an urban
character without
denying its modernity.

Opposite page,
the work draws a line
between the two towns.
The varying beam
section allows
to control its height.
The roadway thickness
is not visible, only
the fineness
of the pedestrian
pathway shows.

Daniel Faucher University Campus

SAHLM of University (for low-cost housing)
CROUS – SACIM

This project to redevelop Daniel Faucher University Campus on Ile du Ramier in Toulouse pays careful heed to the old rationalist-style of architecture works. Almost eight hectares for eight buildings catering for a total of one thousand students. Located near sports facilities and the municipal swimming pools, this citadel is the same distance from the old city centre and two main residences, Le Mirail and Paul Sabatier. This was actually the very first university complex to be built after the war in 1949/1950 under the influence of the modern movement. Robert Valle's original design included six 170-room buildings for a total of 1000 students, plus restaurant, administration building, auditorium, and common room. Building work carried on until 1954 without completing the programme (auditorium and common room were never built). A first extension was made in 1960/1964 through the addition of two new buildings (for a further 200 rooms) designed by Fabien Castaing. The rational design of the buildings lets them fit neatly into their surroundings. The east-west layout and proper distancing between the buildings ensures they are well-lit and knit into the landscape. The buildings are notably constructed on piles in accordance with modernist thinking and to ensure the complex does not block the River Garonne when it floods its banks. Key design guidelines included reinforcing the site's main axis (with the buildings set out in a comb shape), focusing on the entrance, compensating for the smallness of the car parks, and re-thinking the system of pedestrian ways. The original layout fits in neatly with the general redevelopment programme designed by Atelier 13: the development of spaces and rearrangement of levels. A detailed project of bookcases, under-bed storage space, wardrobes, and bathroom furniture, are all designed to embellish the accommodation facilities. The interiors also extend outside through the loggias. The outside walls are made entirely of brick in the case of the first six buildings and partly of brick for the other two, with exposed concrete for the remaining parts.

The directing scheme project features a variety of accommodation facilities ranging from bed-sitters to one-and two-roomed flats, the re-organisation of the road network, a new system of pedestrian ways, and a new outside lighting system. The project is built in lots. Although the original layout has been complied with and enhanced, great care has also been paid to providing maximum comfort, building precision, and cutting-edge plant-engineering (stylistic effects, heat insulation, sound insulation, safety). Attention has mainly been focused on how to use the premises by knitting together the furniture and spaces, providing plenty of storage space, and making practical use of the loggias. The trickiest problem of all was to incorporate the built premises into the landscaping and outside spaces. This called for in-depth knowledge of every single building and their specific tructural/morphological problems. Full-scale restructuring has been carried out, conserving only the bearing sections and creating a radical new layout of space. All the fittings have been replaced and double-glazing fitted. The original "T"-shaped iron sections have been reinserted in the corridors connecting the flights of stairs to the main buildings. The loggia banisters have also been replaced.
A sculptor, N. Kouvaras, was commissioned to work on the central public loggia, while landscape designers from API Paysage also helped with the project.

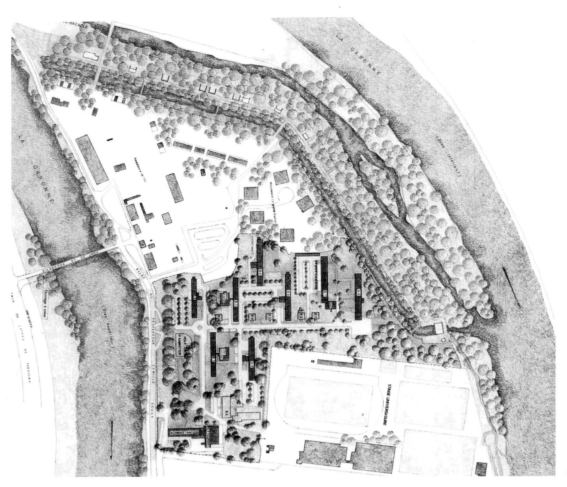

This page, after demolition of all inside partitions, the new building is recomposed with studios. The railings and steel elements were redesigned, while the concrete and brick structure was restructured. Opposite page, heating system.

Site plan.

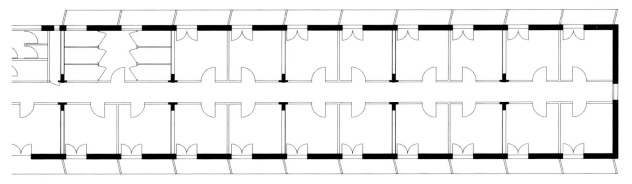

These pages, thanks to the building restoration, the housing typology has been reviewed. The joining of 2 or 3 rooms has allowed to create some studios on 2 frames, or some units consisting of 2 rooms around a bathroom - kitchenette on 3 frames.

Storey floor, before works.

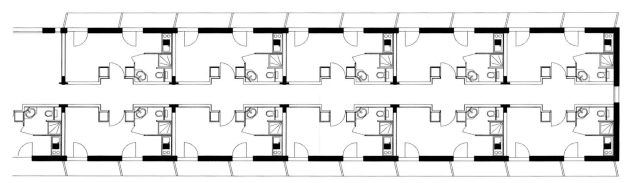

Building restructured, after works.

Above, buildings are erected on piles, with a concrete structure and brick walls. Opposite page, the staircase volume is thus separated from the lodging. Fine door and windows frames maintain the building's character.

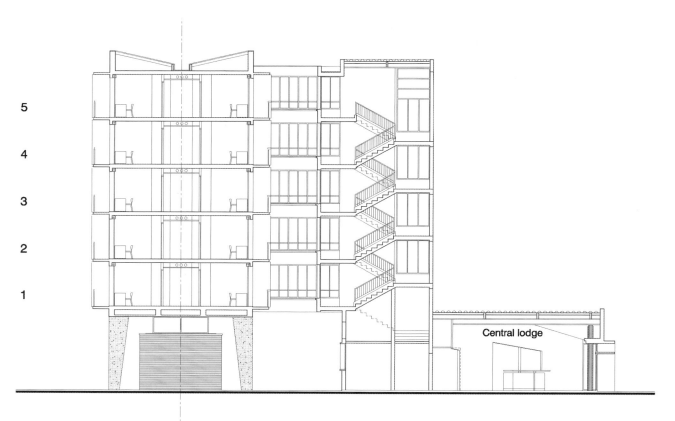

5

4

3

2

1

Central lodge

Cross section.

Bellevue
School Complex

Midi Pyrenees Regional Council
Haute Garonne County Council

The Bellevue School Complex, a huge area of 30 hectares full of vegetation and stretching over different levels, holds a high school, LEP and junior school and stands opposite the Rangueil University Campus.

The entire complex is composed of nine buildings involved in an overall redevelopment, modernisation and extension project. The 1950s' buildings, designed by Camille Montagné for the 1932 Grand Prix de Rome, have been modernised, while the buildings dating back to 1968 have actually been knocked down. The rationalisation and redistribution of functions has led to the construction of offices for the administration and CDI, Research and Documentation Centre, classrooms and laboratories, as well as a restaurant and four office buildings.

The architecture converses here with the landscape and new buildings slot in amidst those already there to create a sense of continuity rather than fracture.

Working on an interesting context, full of trees to be safeguarded, and bearing in mind the orography of the land with its notable height differences, the architecture followed clear guidelines. The two newly designed buildings, constructed around a collective space, "move through the trees" adapting to them and respecting them. The movements of the land, carefully rendered in the form of terraces and steps, accompany the new buildings.

A concrete portico stretches for eighty metres and links together the buildings, instilling a general sense of unity which, at nighttime, transforms itself (thanks to clever use of lighting by Atelier 13) into a long procession of spotlights.

The new architecture converses with the 1950s' buildings. The vocabulary of bricks and concrete, the interplay of transparencies, visual perceptions, treatment of outside space, and porticoes, all help to make this work of architecture a system open to paths and discoveries, where nature is ever-present.

The restaurant over on the most dominant area of the site is highly distinctive and easy to recognise, acting as a sort of observation deck across the surroundings and offering an interesting view point. Built on a circular site plan, it is surrounded by a communication trench and also holds a restaurant room carefully designed in terms of both light and materials.

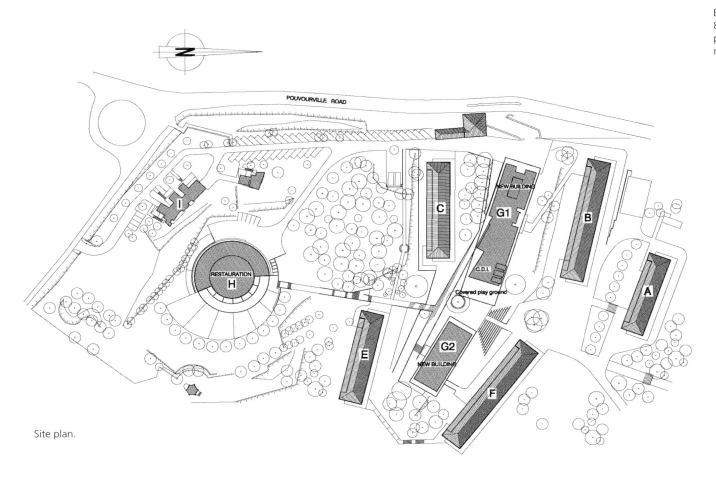

Site plan.

The circular restaurant towers the site. It perfectly suits the site and is characterized by a play of deactivated concrete pathways which connect it to all the other College buildings.

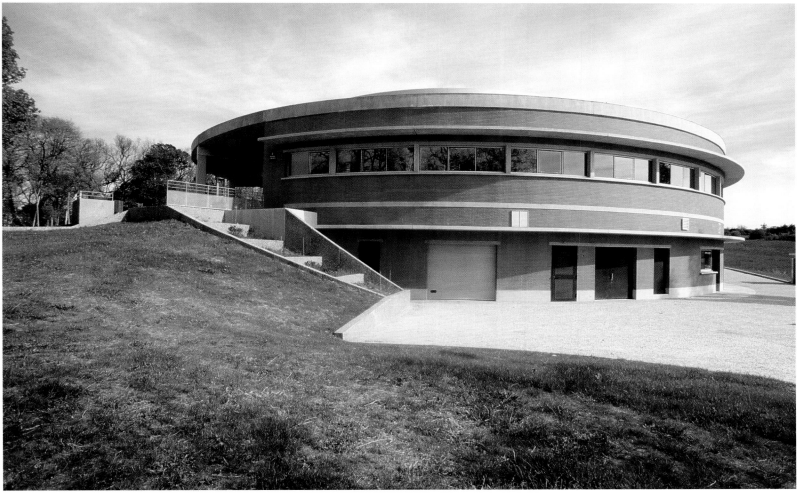

Opposite page, the arcade ensures the connection between the two bodies of the building. It underlines the porch and gives a built character to the external spaces. It plays with shade and light both day and night.

Riglit, the building is realized in sand coated light concrete. The pile rhythms play with light. Below, the Documentation Center distinguishes itself by its vertical skylights.

Below,
the Documentation
and Information Center
with its natural
overhead lighting.

Opposite page, student
restaurant. It is realized
on a circular base and
provides a panoramic
view. Its perimeter
is encircled by concrete
arcades. The steel
structure is made
of engraved metal
beams and the central
post is subtended
by steel cables.
Sound treatment
is ensured between
the beams by means
of a tensioned cloth.

52 Apartments

The project for this housing complex involves a total of 52 apartments, including 14 one-room units, 23 two-room units, 9 three-room units, and 6 four- or five-room units. Despite the complexity of the main structure in relation to the lie of the land, the rational site plan allows the surface area of each level to be exploited as effectively as possible so that ten apartments can be served by one single unit of stairs and lifts. Situated on strongly sloping land (a height difference of over 25 metres), the complex is constructed in steps and follows the lie of the embankment on which it is built.

The main building, basically symmetrical to the main axis, envelops a vertical glass and concrete structure holding the stairs serving all the different floors. This 25-metre-tall element is detached from the construction enveloping it, acting as a neighbourhood landmark during both the day (thanks to its different materials) and night (acting like a kind of lantern).

The building also stands out for the way it knits into the web of urban pathways, intertwining with the building's pathways, passages, porticoes, clearings and plazas.

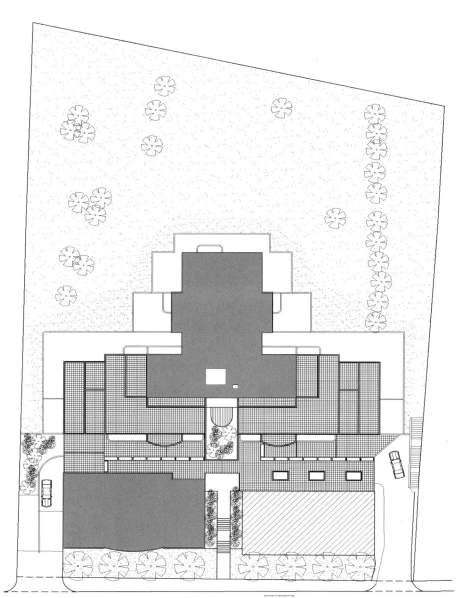

Along the road
boundaries the building
offers a series
of terraces, thus giving
the visitor different path
possibilities and
unexpected spaces.
Bottom, the central
staircase glass column
and a play of walkways
can be made out.

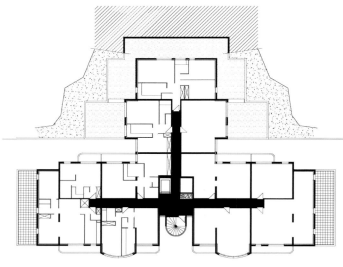

Ground floor plan.

Site plan.

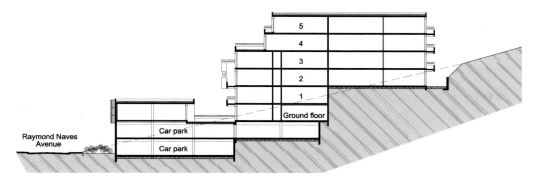

| 5 |
| 4 |
| 3 |
| 2 |
| 1 |
| Ground floor |

Raymond Naves Avenue

| Car park |
| Car park |

Transversal section.

The big white facade which opens on a hanging garden. The urban landscape stretches off into the distance. All apartments have a terrace.

Conference Centre

City of Toulouse
SETOMIP

Associate architect
M. Commissaire

This is a conference building strategically located in relation to Toulouse city centre. The building, near of the Capitole Place, contributes through its own powerful image to give a new function to the Compans-Caffarelli's plot. This newly designed building is composed of three above-ground level, including a double-height amphitheatre, and an underground level. The structural layout and the way this affects how the building is perceived from the outside are clearly based around the idea of balanced fronts and interaction with the surroundings, rather than a rather conventional hierarchical arrangement of main and secondary facades. In contrast, here it is the part of the building hinging around the public park at the back of the auditorium that provides the most interesting feature of the interaction with the landscaping.
A large full-height glass house, inside and integrated in the building, mediates the transition from the park to the construction's built architecture. This creates a sort of "boundary" between interior and exterior, drawing on both the garden features of the outdoor environment and bordered space and comfort of the interiors. The separation of this environment from the outside is entrusted to an aesthetically/stylistically striking full-height glass partition, standing out for the lightness and transparency of its design. This glass wall is arranged to bring out the structure's horizontality, even though it is actually set back from the smooth plane of frameless glass panels. The glass is actually designed to structure the facade, using it vertically to connect to the under-structure's main frame made of iron tubes painted white. The glass house is counterbalanced by a structure flanking the main building clad with pre-oxidised copper and holding the escalators and entrances. Glass reappears again outside and is designed to create transparent squares on glossed backgrounds, also featuring a decorative structure sloping by the entrance hall, where overhead glass also provides zenith lighting. The sloping section plays stylistically with the system of ramps leading off from the stairs.
The underground level can hold 1200 people. The amphitheatre, extending between the first and second floors is designed for 500 people, while other rooms and small premises are cut to provide seating for between 50-300. A 800 (300+500)-place restaurant completes the range of different services and facilities.

The building occupies a plot in the middle of an existing little islet. Two strong ideas have been developed: the dialogue between the building and the Park, by means of the big greenhouse, and the image of public building, given by the facade stairs which can be seen from the Boulevard.

Above right, detail of the facade's under structure made of iron tubes painted white.

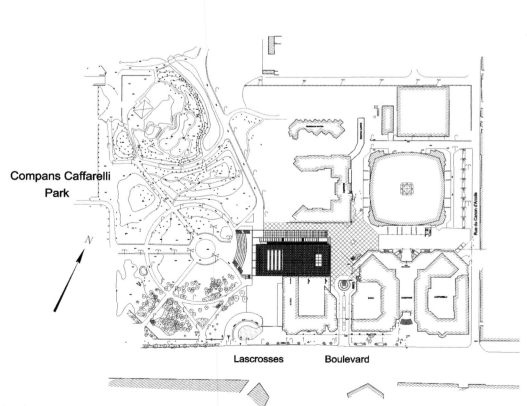

Compans Caffarelli
Park

N

Lascrosses   Boulevard

Site plan.

The large full-height
glass perimeter mediates
the transition from the
park to the architecture
inside.

Left, the 500-seat amphitheatre has beech panel cladded walls. A series of control rooms are located at the rear of the hall. Every two rows the specifically designed seats are equipped with folding tablets which can host a computer.

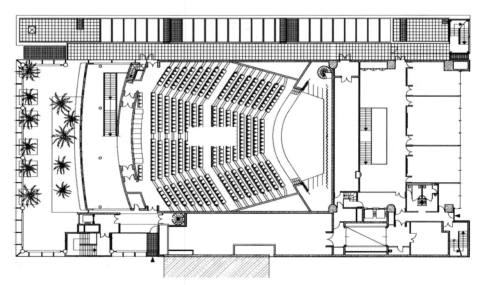

Third floor plan.

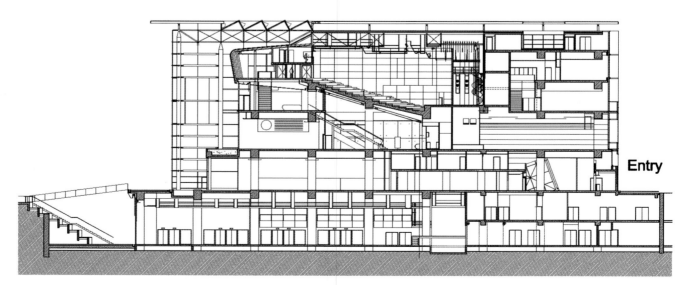

Entry

Longitudinal section.

Left, the space scale difference creates a surprise effect. Here is a double height. The raw materials, such as the concrete, oppose the marble panels. Below, the entrance hall. At the mezzanine floor the meeting point café and the glass-gallery which leads to the lower floor can be made out.

Opposite page, in order to better understand the building, all escalators follow one another and cross the various floors. Fire escapes and elevators are located at the two ends.

Below, night view of the building, which stands out as a luminous landmark.

CROUS' Headquarters

You need to know all about a historical building before you can work on it properly. This assumption lies at the very foundation of Atelier 13's project to reorganise part of the building situated right in the heart of Toulouse's old city centre, relocating the different services of the Crous' new headquarters. The complex involves an area of 7,000 square metres surrounded on three sides by urban roads and features a 60-metre facade along Rue du Taur.

The block can be accessed through a large open gate extending into the old building's courtyard of honour. The original site plan dates back to the 14th century when Perigord College was first built. The first little seminary was set up in the 18th century. Important works in the 19th century left it looking as it does now: an Imperial-style brick building constructed around a courtyard. A series of full arches on the ground floor create a cloister.

The complex has been the home to the university, General Affairs, and student accommodation since 1906. This final section has been furbished with rooms for Crous and the O.T.U.'s student travel agency.

On a functional level, the main purpose was to group the various facilities, student aid management and computer services in one single place.

The project covers 2,500 square metres over four levels.

The ground floor holds the entrance with its own hall and large meeting room, and the O.T.U. travel agency. The first floor contains services related with student life, grants, accommodation and social services.

The second floor holds the financial/computer services and cultural facilities. The third floor is home to the human resources directors and executives.

Working on the assumption that you need in-depth knowledge of the building being worked on, preliminary research, historical inquiry and surveying had to be carried out. The idea was to gauge the complex's intrinsic qualities: brick walls, panelled ceilings, full arches, and spacious interiors. The architects then incorporated the main cores instilling a certain rigidity to constrain the site plan, notably the entrances, stairs, and toilettes, leaving plenty of room for any later adjustments. This means the spaces have been carefully adapted to the real nature of the complex.

The central building was clearly the most obvious place to hold the entrance and reception facilities. The need for considerable natural direct lighting resulted in the creation of a large gap in the old building's brick wall.

Two large exposed reinforced concrete columns hold up a twelve-metre steel architrave. Inside there is a nice blend of open spaces and private offices. Different floors serve different purposes. There is plenty of stone cast-on-site concrete with brass joints in the entrance hall and meeting rooms, and raised floors in the computer rooms with wood or linoleum finishes. Special attention has been reserved for the three stairways.

The main stairs start in marble grit and concrete and terminate in a lighter steel structure and wooden steps. The flight of steps hinging together the two buildings is suspended in space and has no supporting perimeter walls. It is made entirely of steel and wood with exits at different levels via walkways. The stairs connected to the mezzanine in the O.T.U. offices have steel steps designed along minimalist lines. The lighting is designed out of a combination of natural and artificial light to serve both practical and decorative requirements. The artificial light is supposed to bring out the spatial features of the premises. The use of red brick, exposed concrete, and light and dark wood, help inject the spaces with their own definite identity.

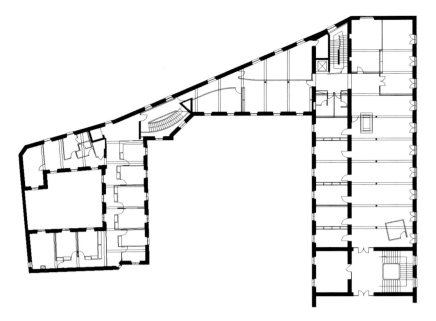

Second floor plan.

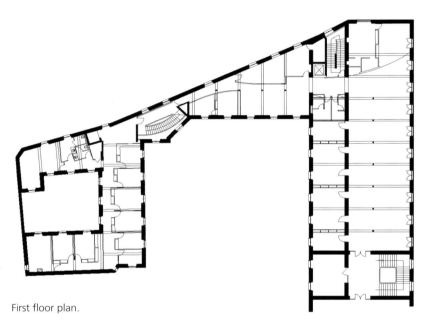

First floor plan.

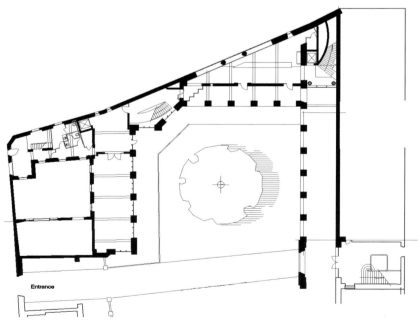

Ground floor plan.

Below, view of the building, which is located in a historical area. It was important to take into due consideration its treasures - beams, brick walls, arched windows etc. and to provide living comfort to the new spaces.

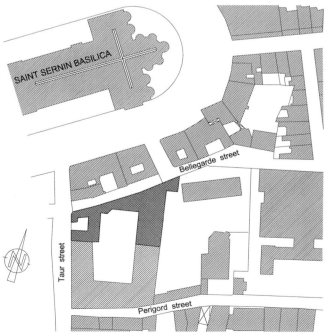

Site plan.

Views of the renovated interior spaces.
To have light entering the building thickness was the first goal: translucent partition walls, re-opening of windows and doors, specific light studies.

Section on the courtyard.

These pages, as a consequence of the hall hinging between the 2 building bodies, the choice of a large opening into the brick facade has been made. With its 12m length, the steel beam which lies on 2 concrete drums supports the heavy facade. Natural light enters the hall.

The connection between the 2 building bodies has been the occasion for setting transparences: alternation of sanded and light walls – exterior-interior views.

Below, detail of the
interior, where old
and new materials
are combined.
Opposite page,
the stairs are located in
a 2-volume articulation.
It is suspended in space
by steel bars hanging
from the ceiling.
At each floor, some
wooden walkways allow
to enter the premises.
Steps and banisters
are made of wood.

Agricultural High School

Midi Pyrenees Regional Council
COGEMIP

Atelier 13 was asked to design a small approximately 800-square-metre girls' boarding facility inside a complex housing a high school. The building is furbished with eight rooms with four beds, their own bathroom facilities and another separate room. In addition to the sleeping quarters, the building also has communal facilities including a sick bay, cloakroom and study room. The project, which takes the place of an old building that has been knocked down, is designed like a brick building with a porticoed area. This portico calls to mind the imposing grandeur of a Renaissance design, embracing both levels of the building. There are windows up on the first floor where the apartments are located and "eyes" or round windows on the ground floor serving the communal spaces.

The use of the materials Atelier 13 has opted for the overall building design ensure the building fits in with the surrounding 19th-century buildings.

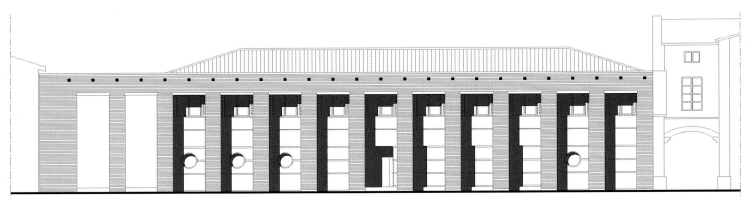

South elevation.

Above and opposite page, the large brick arcade ensures the connection between the 2 courtyard spaces, thereby providing a special nobleness to the new area.

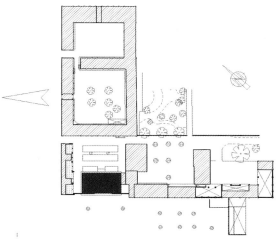

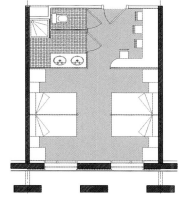

Site plan.

Typical 4-bed bedroom.

Arnaud Bernard Square

This project was directly commissioned by the general public itself, as the local community expressed its desire to see the main square redesigned and redeveloped. The key inputs guiding the design work were ease of access for business concerns and an overall refurbishing of the square to cater for a wide range of different needs. This included access to the old underground car park, maintaining room for activities already held in the square such as a book fair and tango festival, and ensuring emergency services could still get to the square.

The trapezium-shaped square covers 4,500 square metres with its shortest side opening onto a large crossroads. The underground section holds a 270-space car park with a ticket booth and lift at ground level.

The project was designed around a number of guidelines. Most importantly, the need to level out the place into one single space and keep as much traffic out of the square as possible. A surface structure designed to provide access to the underground car park was replaced by a glass kiosk holding the lift. The impact of the ramp leading into the car park was also softened down. As usual, Atelier 13 paid careful attention to lighting, opting for a spattering of light clearly marking the square and making it look cheerful at night.

The need to furbish the square for various purposes encouraged the architects to pay careful attention to the choice of materials for the paving and furbishing, chosen for their durability and expected to be highly unlikely to cause safety problems (slip-proof). The paving is made of deactivated concrete, gravel from the Garonne alternating with strips of porphyry to link together the two facades facing the square. The paths are made of granite blocks, while the car park ramps are made of concrete and granite. The porter's lodges are made of stainless steel and the lift is all-glass. The lift is actually custom-made for this project, as are other furbishing features such as the bumps in the road to slow traffic and the benches made of wood and cast iron. The lighting appliances are made of aluminium and polycarbonate.

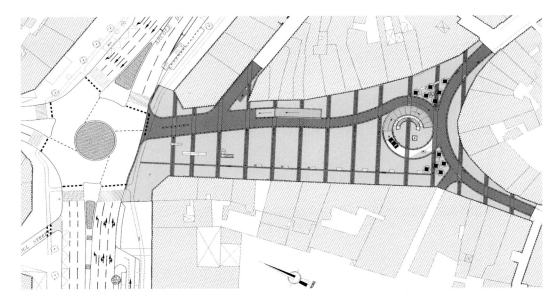

The place has different uses: neighborhood service, underground parking, local market or ball place.
Cast iron posts channel the cars.

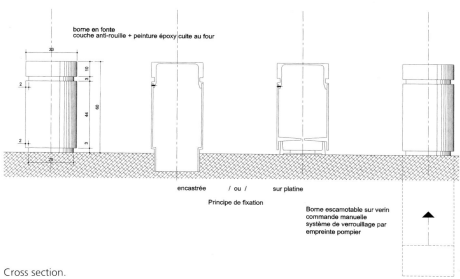

borne en fonte
couche anti-rouille + peinture époxy cuite au four

encastrée / ou / sur platine

Principe de fixation

Borne escamotable sur verin
commande manuelle
système de verrouillage par
empreinte pompier

Cross section.

Below, like shining
wands, the lamp posts
confers a poetic touch
to the night.

Saint Paul's Parish Church

Toulouse Diocese
Saint Paul's Parish Church

A building once used as a mechanical workshop and then converted into Saint Paul's Parish Church has been fully refurbished to bring its architecture up-to-date without altering its function. Of course, there was nothing on the outside of the building to indicate it was a place of worship, so the refurbishing provided the chance to make the parish church a local landmark and give the community a greater sense of belonging.

The first decision to be made was to place a large cross on the facade. Its careful design and the use of unexpected materials such as rusty steel and copper provided an interesting contrast with the brick facade.

The congregation space in the chapel has been given special attention. A churchyard with steps leads from the road to the entrance gate. It is made of concrete in a variety of aggregates. The steps are eye-catching thanks to the use of brick edges, while the highest level features geometric patterns made of a combination of coloured glass, brick and tiles.

Life has been injected in the flooring by the sculptor N. Kouvaras. The main entrance calls to mind the cross through the same use of rusted steel and small inlays of steel and coloured glass.

The windows are given an old-fashioned look by alternating sanded and blue-and-yellow glass designed to recreate the characteristic atmosphere of traditional places of worship.

The rather bland and uninspiring interiors badly needed to be refurbished. The idea was to make this place of worship as dignified looking as possible. All kinds of work was carried out. A special heating system was fitted to make the place more comfortable.

Work on the space and light was, of course, of fundamental importance. The altar was relocated to get it more actively involved in the chapel as a whole, placing it on a large stage made of clear wood and creating a feeling of separation from the deep blue diagonal wall forming the backdrop. The wall also conceals the entrance to the vestry. Little spotlights act like large star-spangled "paintings" also helping support the tabernacle. A large white cross stands out from the background.

The lighting is designed along two different lines: the soft light from the opal glass wall lamp combines with the lovely light from the blue and yellow glass windows literally transforming the interior space.

Small projectors highlight the *terracotta* statues in the white niches formed by the old apertures in the brick walls uncovered beneath the plaster. The old grey concrete flooring has been replaced by a *terracotta* floor. Kouvaras has designed a sculpture made of glass sprinkled with gold, blue or rust, white and green marble, and threads of brass, to add deeper meaning to this place of worship.

These works give a greater sense of character and dignity that was previously lacking. Saint Paul's Parish Church is now a real landmark for the local community.

The big rusty steel and copper cross plays the signal role.
The entrance portal – made of the same materials – matches the glass windows (yellow, blue and opalescent glass).

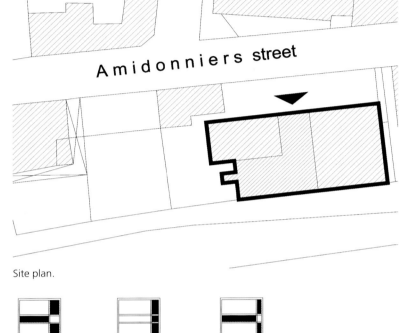

Site plan.

A B C D E F G

Stained, glass windows.

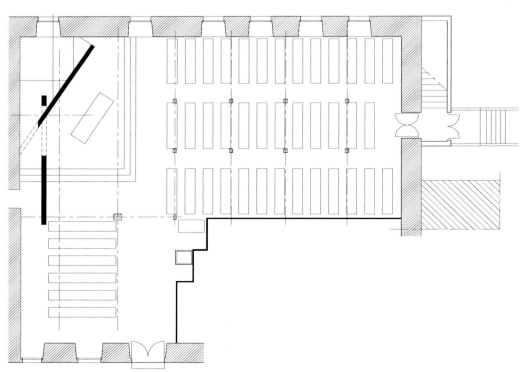

Main floor plan.

Left, detail of the copper cross.
Below, two blue walls with a white cross intersect, thereby staging the altar.

The Miller's House

SAHLM of University (for low-cost housing)
"The Garden City" – Blagnac

The community remembers it as the "Miller's house". It is a large building with brick walls whose visually striking presence deeply entrenched in its context called for great care and intelligence in being redeveloped. The project also involved an adjoining construction. Thanks to the renovation work, the complex now holds nine flats and a chemist's, while two new flats have been built on the edge of the site. The key theme is to salvage an important piece of the local architectural heritage, altering its use and making it comfortable to live in, in accordance with its future inhabitants' expectations. This called for carefully designed new openings in the facade and a site plan of meticulous precision. The painted wooden fixtures are custom-made, as are the facade with its big steel girder and the portico made of woven steel.

The flats are all different and are tailor-made for two or three inhabitants. There are also a number of duplex apartments. This project shows how the old and new can successfully co-exist.

This page, on the new openings, whether created, enlarged, hidden or protected by grids, an important work had been made: the rusty steel twisted portal; right, composed openings, following the steel beam laying. Thanks to the natural lime based coating the brick frames can be made out.

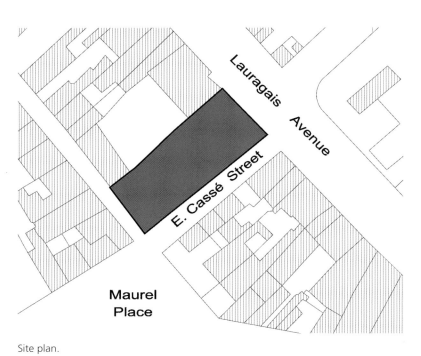

Site plan.

Detail of the renovated facade.

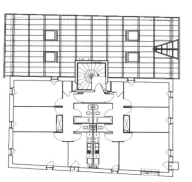

Third floor plan.

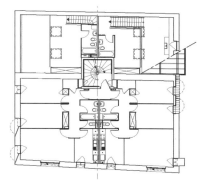

Second floor plan.

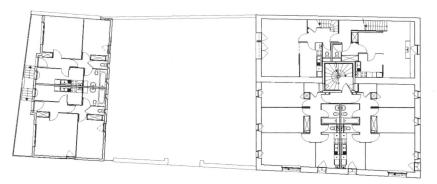

First floor plan.

Parking

Shop

Ground floor plan.

Students Residences

University Work Regional Centre
CROUS

This project involved completely redeveloping an old building in the historical city centre of Toulouse. The 83 existing rooms were converted into 62 studios, each with its own cooking area and bathroom facilities. Adopting a rather conventional approach to this kind of project, Atelier 13 focused with great accuracy on the minor details, including the incorporating of furniture specially designed to fit in with the architecture. A painted oxidised steel entrance gate was constructed along Rue Bellegarde to redevelop the area right alongside the building and help incorporate the project in its micro-urban setting. The entrance is through a steel and wood walkway constructed over a white gravel path flanked by a row of cypress trees.

The old city and old surroundings are carefully respected through in the materials used, which range from rusted iron to brick, gravel and wood. Stylistically speaking this is a classical design featuring a straight central corridor leading out of both sides of the living quarters arranged in a line to make the most rational possible use of the building fronts.

Above, the entrance to the renovated building, in which the original rooms have been transformed into newly designed studios.

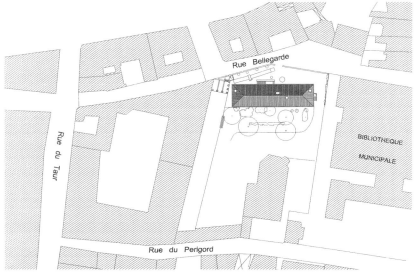

 Site plan.

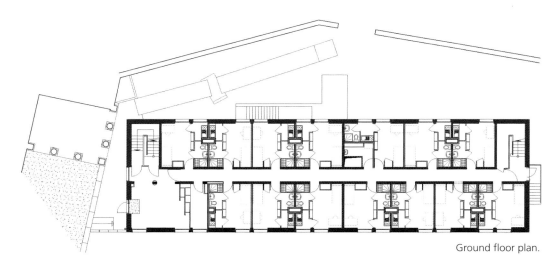

Ground floor plan.

All furniture inside the apartments is perfectly integrated and specifically designed: bookcase, storage units, toilet tables, etc …

Jean Jaurès Station, Metro Line B

Toulouse Agglomeration Subway - SMAT - SMTC

Associate architects
SCP de Capèle - Lamarque

J ean Jaurès Station with its busy flow of passengers is the exchange
station between Lines A and B on the Toulouse underground system.
Preliminary studies envisaged a tunnel link between the two lines,
as well as another tunnel connection to the shopping precinct
incorporated in the same junction.

Atelier 13's project works on the station's strategic role to set new goals
and expectations. The connection between the two lines develops through
a huge junction and a shopping precinct.

The station has three platforms and is also superimposed over Line A.
The overall project involves a re-thinking of all the public space, including
the outside areas. This means the entire Roosevelt block has been altered
and the traffic reorganised. This makes the project an authentic urban design.
Of all the rail traffic facilities, the junction room with its huge columns plays
a signature role, further enhanced by its huge flat glass roof. The station
is designed on a three-platform scheme. A mezzanine equipped with three
glass lifts connects the three walkways above the lines. The station ceiling
is made of reinforced concrete panels.

Structures and space, light and pathways, these are the design concepts
underpinning this important and complex infrastructural junction from
the start.

This project is designed to fit in with the old line, thereby enhancing
the identity and unitary nature of the entire system, partly by drawing
on homogeneous graphic elements, morphological features and materials.

Opposite page, station develops on double height, with 3 platforms. Travellers walk along the walkways located above the trains. They are able to anticipate their routes and orientate themselves easily.

Line B is located above the existing Line A. Jean Jaurès, the station which connects the 2 lines, features a big double-angled glass house with shopping mall and an exchange room. This space serves as a connection between the two lines.

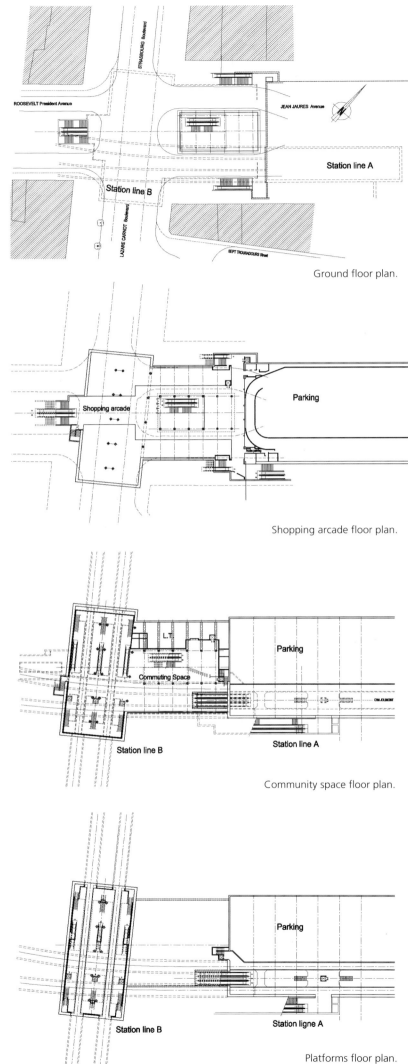

Ground floor plan.

Shopping arcade floor plan.

Community space floor plan.

Platforms floor plan.

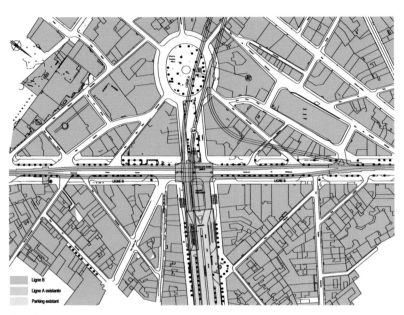

Site plan.

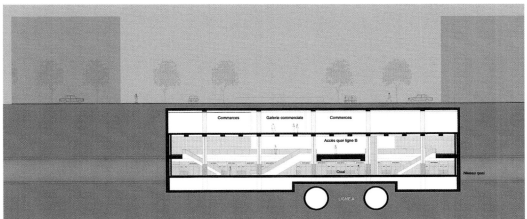

Strasbourg Boulevard

Shopping arcade

Mezzanine

Line B

Line A

Commuting Space

Parking

Longitudinal Section

D.D.A.S.S. Offices

T he building is designed to house the offices and services of the Direction Départmentale de l'Action Sanitaire et Sociale, and is divided into office spaces, communal services, meeting and congregation spaces, and covered parking spaces. The architectural complex's image is mainly determined by the fifty-metre-long road facade featuring vertical glass screens.

These screens are counterbalanced by a base made of stone, the same material used for some of the grounding fixtures. The building is divided into three strips with the services located in the center, freeing space for offices along the facades. This architecturally clean and clear-cut building is pleasant to inhabit thanks to the scale and proportions of its various subdivisions. The floors of the various levels jut out of both sides of the building's vertical perimeter, marking the design horizontally. It is this overhanging part of the floors that holds the glass screens facing east and hence inclined in relation to the two main building axes. The building has four stories above ground level, including a smaller top floor holding a large meeting room surrounded by a balcony.

Top and above, the facade which overlooks the boulevard is equipped with noise and sunshine glass screens. A canopy marks the entrance and underlines the base, and the last floor is slightly set back from the facade.

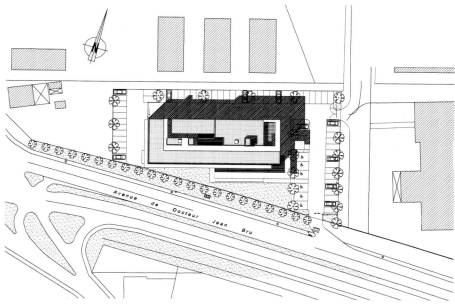

Site plan.

Above, the entrance hall
and the meeting room.
Left, detail of the
sunshine glass screens.

Profile of Firm

by Nicole Roux Loupiac
and Jean Philippe Loupiac

We began studying at the Toulouse School of Architecture in 1966, where we received a "Fine Arts"-type education. We then continued our architectural studies after the 1968 events in Paris – Teaching Unit n° 1 – and, at the same time, we followed a course at the Engineering Institute – Industrial Methods of Architecture – and at the Town-Planning Institute, Paris VIII, Vincennes with Pierre Merlin and Françoise Choay. During that period architecture was opening up to other fields and we could no longer treat it as an independent discipline.

Two years under Jean Prouvé at the CNAM – Centre National des Arts et Métiers – taught us that very often an excellent architectural design is also an excellent technical solution. The two approaches merge.

With him we discovered the erudite learning of Maillard's construction works.

So where does architecture begin and technique end?

There is actually just one overall solution. Artistry derives from both architecture and technique. There must be a certain coherence between the two.

This was the spirit of experimental research in which we prepared our master's degree in town-planning.

Our master's degree also gave us the chance to meet the biologist and philosopher Henri Laborit, who is deeply concerned about the way people's aggressiveness builds up inside built spaces and has certainly influenced us: "before thinking about architecture, think about people, put them at the centre of everything".

This is a way of remaining faithful to yourself and of meeting the basic goals of architecture.

In July 1973 we won a town-planning competition and shortly afterwards we set up Atelier 13 in Paris. We took part in lots of competitions and in October of the same year we entered our PAN 5 – Programme Architecture Nouvelle – Medium-sized Cities in an ideas competition launched by the Ministry of Public Works for young architects, whose theme was housing and which we actually managed to win. We focused our work on housing until the early-1980s.

In 1975 we opened an agency in Toulouse and we eventually left the capital in 1982. We soon set up a team, since we feel that architecture is not a solitary act but a profession calling for a constant exchange of opinions.

We are absolutely convinced we are links in a chain. The complexity of the city or certain projects makes us organise multi-disciplinary teams with outside consultants. This is the only way various points of view on problematic design issues will emerge. But we also feel that the client and company ought to perform different roles without interfering with each other.

Our initial experience convinced us of the following points:
1. Architecture always has its own site (cityscape, natural setting etc…).
2. Architecture's relation to context is fundamental in as far as it gives it meaning.
3. What is really at stake is not in architecture but in the composition or recomposition of territories. This means it must be viewed on different scales.
4. Architecture is designed for people, spaces can generate feelings. This means architecture must move beyond mere utility – poetry of space, structures, materials, colours, light.
5. Architecture turns out to be an intellectual act deriving from thought. It conveys meaning but is also an act imposed by matter. Controlling building work and construction details is a real struggle. Coherence derives from controlling a project and how it is carried out.

By definition, architecture involves parameters of different kinds: needs; site location; constraints due to regulations; construction site requirements.

The solution must be more than just the applying of parameters.

Success is something more than the sum of these elements.

It is the attempt to create relations between separate elements to produce meaning.

Architecture and experimentation are closely linked. Doing architecture means looking for the right answer, searching for truth or, in other words, seeking out your very self.

Doing architecture or town-planning means giving shape to a vision of the world and organising the world in which we live, viz., it means trying to inject it with coherence. We need to think in terms of TIME.

List of Works

Social and Private Residences

1975-1980
Epinal - Vosges
200 apartments at Epinal - Shops
and parking spaces
as per the New Architecture Programme
Competition 1974

1976
Castanet - Haute Garonne
Houses complex and intermediate 150 houses
CREPAH - Société de Crédit Immobilier de
Toulouse et du Sud Ouest
Société Anonyme d'HLM "La Cité Jardins"
Competition

1981
Larramet Neighbourhood - Toulouse
80 individual houses complex
GBA 3 concrete construction system
Public Office HLM Toulouse

1984
Rue Mamy - 25 Community Residences
Public Municipal Office HLM Toulouse
Brick Constructive system
Work awarded with Palmarès Régional de
l'Habitat
Competition

1989
Rue Rancy - Toulouse
54 social residences and property accession -
sports hall
Promologis - SAMAI

1990
Avenue Raymond Naves - Toulouse
52 collective houses and property accession -
parking spaces
Société Civile Immobilière Bellevue

1994
Saint Orens - Haute Garonne
30 social houses
Société Patrimoine

1998
Rue Sainte Anne - Toulouse
33 collective houses and accession in a
historic area
RUGGIERI Promotion

1999
Tournefeuille - Haute Garonne
68 collective houses in accession
SOGEFI Promotion

Renovation
Residential Sector – Restoration

1990
Cité Empalot - Toulouse
192 residences
Neighbourhood Social Development
Operation
OPAC de Toulouse
1991-1993
Cité Jolimont – Toulouse
289 residences
Restoration and densification
OPAC de Toulouse

1989-2000
Cité Daniel Faucher - Toulouse
920 students' residences
Complete restoration
CROUS - SAHLM de l'Université
Work awarded in 2001 with Palmarès de la
Réhabilitation par le Ministère de la Culture,
de l'Equipement et l'ANAH

1996-1998
Cité du Taur - Toulouse
62 students' residences
Complete restoration
CROUS - SACIM

1996
Castanet - Haute Garonne
11 residences and 1 shop
Reconversion of a former mill in residences
SAHLM de la Cité Jardins

1998
Students' House - Toulouse
National High School of Engineering and
Aeronautics Construction - 155 residences
ENSICA

Urban Reflections and Site Refurbishment

1988-2001
National Centre of Space Studies
Toulouse Spatial Centre
Site of 56 ha - 2,500 people
Master plan and architectural chart
Landscape plan - circulation - staying areas -
paths - lighting

1989-1999
Bellevue School Complex – Toulouse
Site of 30 ha - 3,000 students
Master plan
Conseil Régional Midi Pyrénées

Daniel Faucher University City
7 ha - 1,200 students
Master plan
CROUS - SAHLM de l'Université

Public Buildings

Reconversion - Restoration

1993-1995
CROUS Offices in Toulouse
Regional Center for University and Social
Works
2,500 sq.m
Reconversion of a building
in a historic area

1995-1996
Spatial Clinic in Toulouse
University Hospital Center
National Center of Space Studies - MEDES
Reconversion of a building

1996
Saint Paul's Chapel in Toulouse
Reconversion of a starch industry in a place
for cult in Rue des Amidonniers

Restoration of Château de Fiac - Tarn
and its annexes - Post Cure Center
Lavaur Hospital - SCIC AM0

1997
Restoration of cardio-vasculary surgery
blocks
Regional Hospital Center Toulouse-Rangueil

1998
Surgery Room
For the Midi-Pyrénées Prefecture in a
building of the XVIII century - Toulouse

1990-1999
Bellevue High School - Toulouse
Restoration - refurbisment - sports
installations - classrooms - restauration
Conseil Régional Midi Pyrénées - COGEMIP

1998-2000
Audio-visual University Institute
2,900 sq.m - Rue du Taur
Reconversion of a building in a historic area
Ministère de l'Education Nationale

Reconversion of a building in Employees'
House
University Hospital Center Toulouse-
Rangueil – 3,000 sq.m
Toulouse Hospital

1999-2000
Administrative Restaurant Toulouse
170 places - Total: 1,293 sq.m
Ministère de l'Intérieur

New Buildings

1981-1982
Municipal Offices - Town of Toulouse
10,000 sq.m
conception - construction competition

1985
Offices of the Equipment Technical Studies
Centre - Toulouse
Competition

Agriculture High school - Ondes - Haute
Garonne
Centre de Machinisme
Competition

1988
Decazeville Professional High School
Offices of chaudronnerie
Competition

1990
Municipal Offices at Carbonne
Haute Garonne
Competition

1993-1997
Exploitation Center of A 64 Highway at
Carbonne (Haute Garonne)
Ministère de l'Equipement / DDE 31
Competition

1993-1995
Bellevue Toulouse High School College
Classrooms - restauration - administration
center
Conseil Général Haute Garonne
Competition

1993-1997
Congress Center Toulouse
Town of Toulouse - SETOMIP
18,000 sq.m
associated: M. Commissaire
Competition

1997-2001
Centre Associatif Enfance Jeunesse
Sports Center at Grenade
Municipality of Grenade sur Garonne
Competition

1998-2000
Offices - Agen - Lot et Garonne
Departmental Direction of the Health
and Social Action
Competition

Infrastructures

1985
Art work on the Dordogne
Sainte Foy la Grande
Competition

1989-1996
Toulouse - Carrefour de Langlade
Echangeur de Bordelongue
Art work along A 64
Toulouse - Muret section
4 new works - 6 refurbished works
Autoroute du Sud de la France - DDE 31
Awarded operation Ruban d'argent au
Palmarès de l'Equipement
Associated: API Paysage
Competition

1994-1997
Bergères Viaduct
Highway A 89
Ussel - Le Sancy Section
Competition

1999-2007
Underground Line B - Toulouse
agglomeration
Architectonic and design chart
Integration chart of art works
Mission d'architecte conseil sur la Ligne B
Associated: Lamarque - de Capèle
Competition

1999-2007
Underground Station Jean Jaurès - Toulouse
Shopping Mall
Commuters junction hall A Line-B Line
Associated: Lamarque – de Capèle

1999-2000
Arnaud Bernard Square - Toulouse
Complete renovation of the square
Access to the underground parking and
circulation
Competition

2001-2002
Roissy Charles de Gaulle Platform
Elaboration of an accessibility
chart for application to the VAL stations